Table of Contents

St. Augustine - the Pirate Target . . 2
John Hawkins 4
Dominique de Gourges 6
Sir Francis Drake 8
Robert Searles 12
Andrew Ranson 14
Nicholas de Grammont 16
Henry Jennings 18
Charles Vane 20
Calico Jack Rackam 22
Francisco Menendez 24
Thomas Bell 26
Louis Aury 28

ABOUT THE AUTHOR - Pat Croce is a New York Times best-selling author, internationally acclaimed speaker, serial entrepreneur, and founder/chairman of the board of the St. Augustine Pirate & Treasure Museum. For more information go to www.thepiratemuseum.com.

SPECIAL THANKS - The author would like to thank the city of St. Augustine's Archaeologist, Carl Halbirt, the Senior Research Librarian at St. Augustine Historical Society, Charles Tingley, and St. Augustine's Director of Heritage Tourism, Dana Ste. Claire, for their valuable insight and research. And to Monte Triz for the rogue portraits and Shaun Aunchman for design of this book.

© 2011 Pat Croce. Published by Historic Print & Map Company, www.historicprint.com

St. Augustine

the Pirate Target

St. Augustine was first explored in 1513 by Spanish explorer, Ponce de Leon, who claimed the region for the Spanish Empire. But it was not until 1565 that the nation's oldest city was established. English pirate John Hawkins inspired the Spanish stronghold when he came to the aid of the French at Fort Caroline and they attacked Spanish vessels in the Caribbean. In response, the Spanish dispatched Admiral Pedro Menendez de Aviles to Florida to establish a base, prevent further French colonization, and protect the Spanish Crown's assets from rogues — particularly their treasure fleets sailing up Florida's eastern seaboard before heading east to Seville.

From 1526, the Spanish ran a highly organized transatlantic convoy system, with two fleets sailing from Seville to the Spanish Americas annually. One fleet landed in Mexico and the other sailed to the Spanish Main on the Caribbean coast of South America where a 200-strong mule train would make its way across the Isthmus of Darien to Panama to pick up Peruvian silver. Both fleets, with holds chock full of silver (70-lb. ingots and pieces of eight), gold doubloons, emeralds, and pearls, would converge in the large Havana port for protection from pirates and to prepare for their journey carrying the plundered wealth of the New World back to the old world.

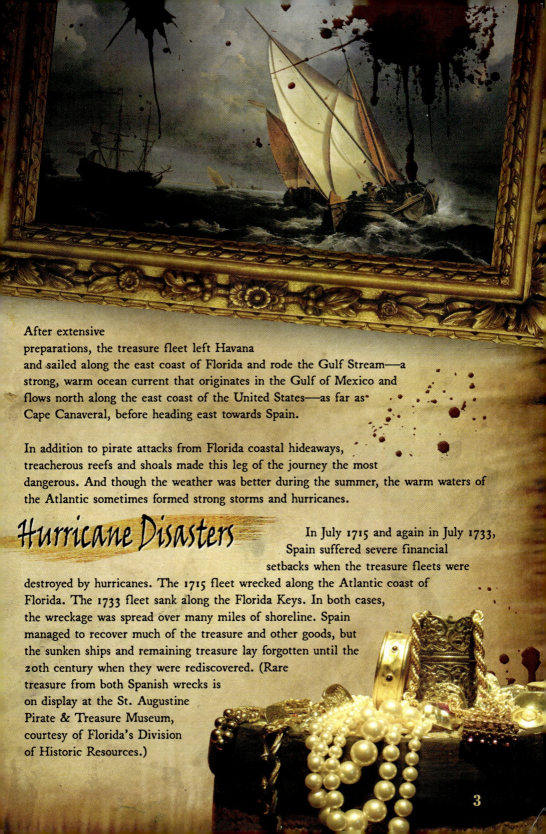

After extensive preparations, the treasure fleet left Havana and sailed along the east coast of Florida and rode the Gulf Stream—a strong, warm ocean current that originates in the Gulf of Mexico and flows north along the east coast of the United States—as far as Cape Canaveral, before heading east towards Spain.

In addition to pirate attacks from Florida coastal hideaways, treacherous reefs and shoals made this leg of the journey the most dangerous. And though the weather was better during the summer, the warm waters of the Atlantic sometimes formed strong storms and hurricanes.

Hurricane Disasters

In July 1715 and again in July 1733, Spain suffered severe financial setbacks when the treasure fleets were destroyed by hurricanes. The 1715 fleet wrecked along the Atlantic coast of Florida. The 1733 fleet sank along the Florida Keys. In both cases, the wreckage was spread over many miles of shoreline. Spain managed to recover much of the treasure and other goods, but the sunken ships and remaining treasure lay forgotten until the 20th century when they were rediscovered. (Rare treasure from both Spanish wrecks is on display at the St. Augustine Pirate & Treasure Museum, courtesy of Florida's Division of Historic Resources.)

John Hawkins

Pirate Saves First New World Colony (1565)

JOHN HAWKINS, the "praying pirate", was employed by the English as a privateer, but considered a pirate and a criminal by the Spanish. Captain Hawkins spent much of his early maritime career as a slave trader and seeker of Spanish treasure. On his journey back to England from the Caribbean in 1565, he sailed up the coast of Florida looking for freshwater supplies and navigated into the St. Johns River. Hawkins found the Fort Caroline settlement near present-day Jacksonville where two hundred Frenchmen had survived without supplies for over a year. Despite conflicts between the English and the French, Hawkins refused to destroy the fort. He sold the French soldiers supplies and held a prayer service for the inhabitants. But now the reinforced Fort Caroline was a threat to the Spanish and their New World territory. It was shortly thereafter that Pedro Menendez was dispatched to eradicate the French, which ultimately led to the founding of St. Augustine.

Fort Caroline

FORT CAROLINE was the first French colony in present-day United States. It was established in 1564 near the mouth of St Johns River in what is now Jacksonville, Florida, as a refuge for Huguenots. Shortly after John Hawkins provided them aid, the fort suffered a surprise dawn attack by the recently appointed Spanish Governor of Florida, Don Pedro Menendez de Aviles. Everyone was massacred except for about 50 women and children, who were taken prisoner.

Articles of Piracy

From the privateering days of John Hawkins through the Golden Age of Piracy (1680-1730), pirate vessels required each crewmember to sign a set of rules or "articles" that were agreed upon before the ship set sail. Many pirates had suffered great abuse under the tyrannical rule of captains in the merchant service or British Royal Navy. As a result, during their adventurous life at sea, pirates wanted to ensure that their rights were protected, that they had an equal vote in all matters, and that they would receive a fair share of the plunder.

1. Every man has a vote in affairs of moment: has equal title to the fresh provisions or strong liquors at any time seized, and use them at pleasure unless a scarcity makes it necessary for the good of all, to vote a retrenchment.

2. If they defrauded the Company to the value of a dollar, in plate, jewels or money, marooning was the punishment.

3. No person to game at cards or dice for money.

4. The lights and candles to be put out at eight o'clock at night. If any of the crew after that hour still remained inclined to drinking, they were to do it on open deck.

5. To keep their piece, pistols and cutlass clean and fit for service.

6. No boy or woman to be allowed among them. If any man was found seducing any of the latter sex, and carried her to sea disguised, he was to suffer Death.

7. To desert the ship or their quarters in battle, was punished by Death or Marooning.

8. No striking another on board, but every man's quarrels to be ended on shore, at sword and pistol.

9. No man to talk of breaking up their way of living till each had a share of £1,000. If, in order to do this, any man should lose a limb or become a cripple in their service, he was to have 800 dollars out of the public stock, and for lesser hurts proportionably.

10. The Captain and Quarter Master to receive two shares of a Prize; the Master, Boatswain & Gunner, one share and a half and other Officers, one and a quarter.

11. The musicians to have rest on the Sabbath day, but the other six days and nights, none without special favour.

Iron and Lead First, Followed by Steel

Unlike privateers — who only attack vessels from nations their king, queen or country is at odds with — pirates have no such limitations. Any vessel is fair game. Once prey is sighted, a majority vote from the crew is all that is required and the hunt begins. "Iron and lead first, followed by steel" is the piratical way. If the prize doesn't surrender, first comes a massive cannonball onslaught from the big guns. Next comes precision musket marksmanship. And finally, the call to board is given and the pirate party swarms the prey's deck, swinging boarding axes, slashing with cutlasses and firing flintlocks.

Dominique de Gourges

Corsair Harasses Florida's Spanish (1567)

Dominique de Gourges set out in 1567 to avenge the deaths of hundreds of Frenchmen near St. Augustine at the hands of the Spanish a couple of years earlier. The Spanish warned its troops to be on guard against "the descent of pirates"; Gourges' three vessels were known to carry the rogues. But the Spaniards did not realize that Gourges would befriend the local Timucuan tribes who were more than willing to help spill Spanish blood. After exacting his revenge, Gourges sailed home to France with captured cannons and artillery and "a large booty of gold, silver, pearls, and merchandise" that the French sailors declared that they found in Florida. Fearing retaliation from King Philip II of Spain against Gourges' conquests, France's boy King, Charles IX, shunned Gourges. Not so with England's Queen Elizabeth. When her Majesty heard of Gourges' deeds against the mutually hated Spanish, she recruited him to enter her service where his honor and favor were restored.

Timucuan Indians

The Timucua may have been the first American natives to see the landing of Juan Ponce de Leon near St. Augustine in 1513. They were originally a large and powerful tribe made up of as many as 35 chiefdoms along the eastern seaboard, particularly in northern Florida and southern Georgia. Though alliances arose between the chiefdoms, the Timucua were never organized into a single unified tribe. Thus their population was reduced significantly over time because of disease, internal conflicts, and wars against Spanish explorers and English colonists.

Pirate Weapons

Unlike the Timucua, who used primitive bows and arrows, spears, wooden clubs, and stone hatchets, pirates violently attacked their prey armed to the teeth with deadly weapons. Pirates wielded cutlasses, boarding axes, flintlock pistols, muskets, blunderbusses, daggers, grenades, and even cannon fire with lethal precision. Since the pirate motto was "no prey, no pay" and the alternative to losing was death by hanging or grievous wounds and painful "surgery", rogues did whatever it took to ensure a reason to win — and celebrate.

Flesh or Fruit Knives

Like the American Indians, pirates usually carried a dagger or knife as part of their everyday wear. Daggers are often referred to as "flesh or fruit knives" in honor of the "skin" they are best at slicing. Relatively small in size, with a straight blade seldom longer than six inches, the dagger was the perfect tool for thrusting and puncturing prey. When not used for enemy bloodletting, daggers were used for all aspects of piratical life — from shipboard chores (slicing lines, repairing sails) to cutting food during meals.

Sir Francis Drake

World's Greatest Pirate Sacks St. Augustine (1586)

After Francis Drake's historic circumnavigation of the world in the *Golden Hind*, his miraculous defeat of the dreaded Spanish armada, and being knighted by the Queen, this English seadog returned to the Caribbean to continue his plundering ways. With his pirate flotilla of approximately 25 ships and 2,300 men, Drake was arguably the most powerful pirate in world history. Although sanctioned by Queen Elizabeth for his "noble" deeds and dubbed the "Prince of Privateers" by fellow Englishmen, Drake was indeed a pirate. In fact, Her Majesty affectionately called him, "My Pyrate." Known as "El Draque", the Dragon, by her rival monarch, King Philip II, Drake was feared by 16th century Spain as one of the most dangerous and despised men at sea.

Archaeologists Unearth Pirate Siege

Evidence of one of the most devastating pirate raids in world history was unearthed in 1998 by archaeologists here in St. Augustine. City Archaeologist Carl Halbirt and his team discovered the proof while excavating along Marine Street. Here, a layer of charcoal some three inches wide was found in the ground under centuries of fill. The thick charcoal layer is what remains of a town that was burned to the ground in 1586; the same time that Sir Francis Drake destroyed the settlement with his barbarous army. Drake's attack was catastrophic.

In 1586, during his devastating attack on the colonial city of St. Augustine, Drake burned everything to the ground, even the wooden fort, leaving charred evidence of his devastation for archaeologists to find more than four centuries later.

After pillaging the town of its valuables, his men burned everything in sight—buildings, a wooden fort, surrounding fields and groves. The resulting bonfire left the charcoal remnants for archaeologists to discover centuries later. In the ashes, excavators found late 1500s pottery, animal bones, and a pewter needle, all dating back to the late 16th century. The artifacts suggest that the townspeople fled moments before Drake's men arrived, leaving nearly everything they owned behind to save their lives.

Golden Hind

Sir Francis Drake made his historic voyage around the world in the *Golden Hind*. The 120-foot, 150-ton, square-rigged galleon was originally named the *Pelican*, but after squashing a mutiny off the coast of South America, Drake renamed her the *Golden Hind*. The powerful vessel had an armament of 22 guns of various sizes. His global adventure took exactly two years, 10 months, and 18 days. The *Golden Hind* returned to England with a hold full of plundered treasure on September 26, 1580, a year before Drake was knighted and six years before he attacked St. Augustine.

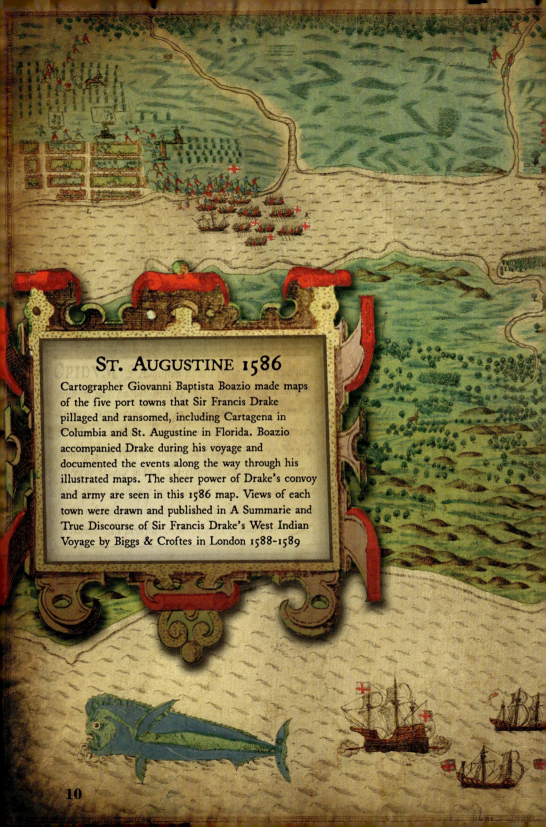

St. Augustine 1586

Cartographer Giovanni Baptista Boazio made maps of the five port towns that Sir Francis Drake pillaged and ransomed, including Cartagena in Columbia and St. Augustine in Florida. Boazio accompanied Drake during his voyage and documented the events along the way through his illustrated maps. The sheer power of Drake's convoy and army are seen in this 1586 map. Views of each town were drawn and published in A Summarie and True Discourse of Sir Francis Drake's West Indian Voyage by Biggs & Croftes in London 1588-1589

Robert Searles

Midnight Raid
Nets Stone Fort (1668)

In May 29, 1668, Captain Searles hid his eight-gun ship Cagway out of sight and sailed a captured Spanish ship into view of the St. Augustine fort. Believing the Spanish vessel was a supply ship from Mexico, the soldiers and townspeople let down their guard. Under the cover of darkness, Captain Searles led his buccaneer crew ashore and sacked the town, raiding the Royal Treasury along the way. Luckily, Governor Francisco de la Guerra y de la Vega made his way to the wooden fort. Searles' band of pirates killed or kidnapped every St. Augustinian they considered to not be of "pure blood". The horrible raid upon her subjects caused Queen Mariana of Spain to finally authorize funding to build the Castillo de San Marcos out of coquina. Searles went on to take part in Sir Henry Morgan's famous sacking of Panama.

Castillo de San Marcos

St. Augustine was founded by Admiral Pedro Menendez de Aviles for the Spanish Crown in 1565. Over the next century, the Spanish built nine wooden forts in various locations to defend the town. After the 1668 attack by English pirate Robert Searles, Queen Mariana of Spain authorized construction of a masonry fortification to protect the city. The fort was built of coquina (which means "little shells"), an almost impenetrable type of stone indigenous to the St. Augustine area that has withstood various attacks, including cannon fire.

Land Attack

Pirates spent the bulk of their time as sea, aboard their ships, searching for prices to plunder. However, from the daring days of John Hawkins, Sir Francis Drake, and Robert Searles, no Spanish city — including St. Augustine - was guaranteed a safe harbor from pirate attack. Where the booty was, the pirates were sure to follow, using whatever means to achieve their goal.

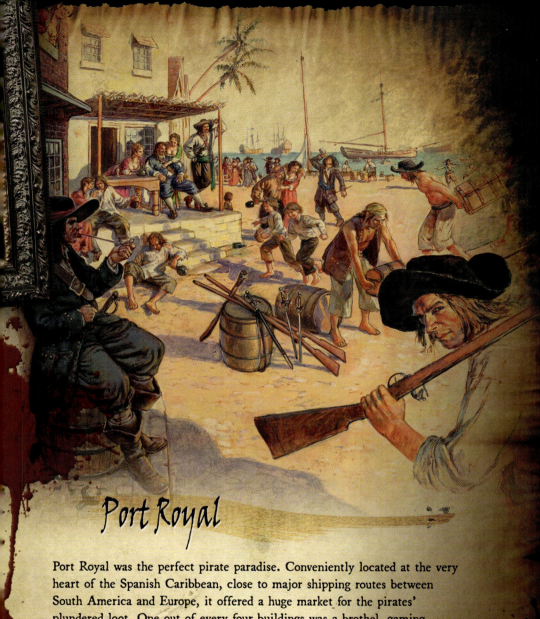

Port Royal

Port Royal was the perfect pirate paradise. Conveniently located at the very heart of the Spanish Caribbean, close to major shipping routes between South America and Europe, it offered a huge market for the pirates' plundered loot. One out of every four buildings was a brothel, gaming house, tavern or grog shop. Port Royal reached its peak of piracy under Sir Thomas Modyford, who as governor ignored England's orders to suppress the Brethren of the Coast and continued to condone the devastating raids on Spanish ships and cities even though war with Spain ended in 1667. With privateering commissions from Modyford, legendary buccaneers like Henry Morgan, Bartholomew Sharp, and Robert Searles sacked Spanish settlements of Maracaibo, Portobello, Panama, and St. Augustine.

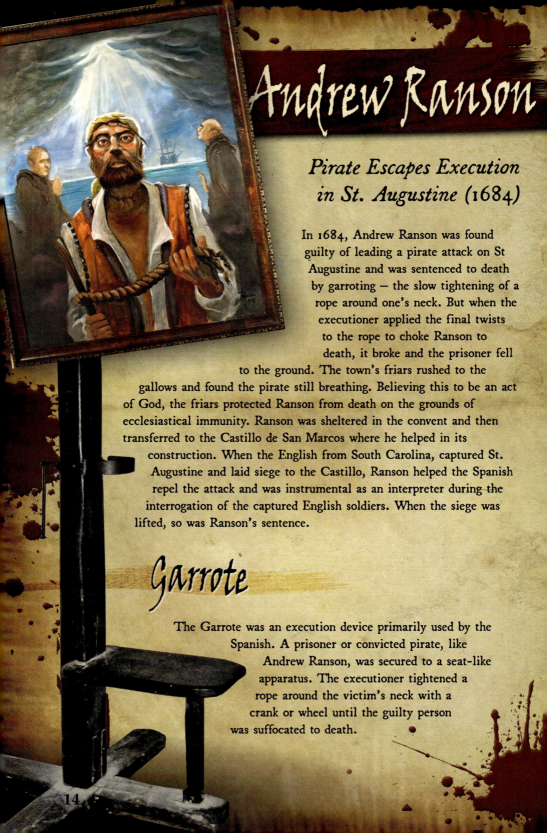

Andrew Ranson

Pirate Escapes Execution in St. Augustine (1684)

In 1684, Andrew Ranson was found guilty of leading a pirate attack on St Augustine and was sentenced to death by garroting — the slow tightening of a rope around one's neck. But when the executioner applied the final twists to the rope to choke Ranson to death, it broke and the prisoner fell to the ground. The town's friars rushed to the gallows and found the pirate still breathing. Believing this to be an act of God, the friars protected Ranson from death on the grounds of ecclesiastical immunity. Ranson was sheltered in the convent and then transferred to the Castillo de San Marcos where he helped in its construction. When the English from South Carolina, captured St. Augustine and laid siege to the Castillo, Ranson helped the Spanish repel the attack and was instrumental as an interpreter during the interrogation of the captured English soldiers. When the siege was lifted, so was Ranson's sentence.

Garrote

The Garrote was an execution device primarily used by the Spanish. A prisoner or convicted pirate, like Andrew Ranson, was secured to a seat-like apparatus. The executioner tightened a rope around the victim's neck with a crank or wheel until the guilty person was suffocated to death.

Death Sentence

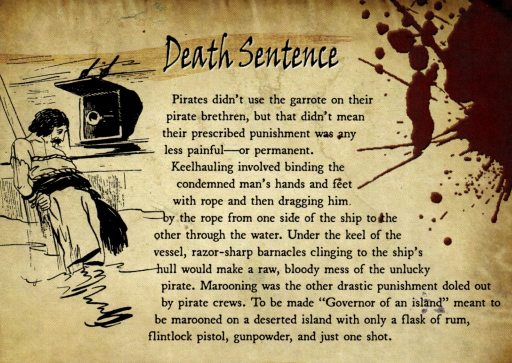

Pirates didn't use the garrote on their pirate brethren, but that didn't mean their prescribed punishment was any less painful—or permanent. Keelhauling involved binding the condemned man's hands and feet with rope and then dragging him by the rope from one side of the ship to the other through the water. Under the keel of the vessel, razor-sharp barnacles clinging to the ship's hull would make a raw, bloody mess of the unlucky pirate. Marooning was the other drastic punishment doled out by pirate crews. To be made "Governor of an island" meant to be marooned on a deserted island with only a flask of rum, flintlock pistol, gunpowder, and just one shot.

First Party to Draw Blood

Fighting amongst the pirate crew was strictly forbidden. Punishment was settled on land, where the antagonists were instructed to fight a duel to the death. If both pirates missed their first shots, they were to immediately resort to swords, and the first party to draw blood was declared the winner.

Nicholas de Grammont

Corsair Blockades Spanish Fort (1686)

Although Le Chevalier Nicholas de Grammont met defeat in 1686 while attempting to lay siege to St. Augustine, this after sacking Vera Cruz, he was a notoriously successful pirate. Under his command, 80 men sailed into Little Matanzas Inlet and seized the watchtower. The Spanish soldiers had killed most of the French forces to the south, but Grammont stayed in the area hoping for reinforcements. Frustrated, he finally abandoned his attack after 16 days and sailed away. But Grammont should have noticed the ring around the moon, telling him of a coming storm. He and his men went down in a devastating hurricane shortly after leaving St. Augustine. While pirate Robert Searles is believed to be the catalyst for the construction of a stone fort at St. Augustine, Grammont's attack is likely the reason the Castillo de San Marcos was completed in 1695 without interruption.

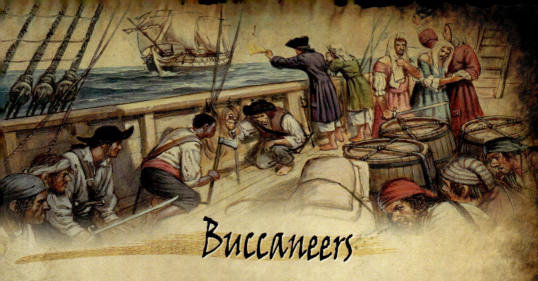

Buccaneers

Buccaneers were pirates who attacked Spanish shipping in the Caribbean Sea and along the mainland of Spanish America during the late 17th century. The word "buccaneer" was derived from the French boucanier, which roughly translates into "someone who smokes meat." Before the Frenchmen were driven away from the island of Tortuga by the Spanish, the buccaneers were expert pig hunters who used "buccans" or wooden frames to smoke the meat. Once set to sea, buccaneers like Henry Morgan, François l'Ollonais, and Nicholas de Grammont laid siege to anything Spanish.

Musket Fire

Since the rise of piracy during the age of buccaneering, the trusty long-barrel musket has been the weapon of choice for long-range hunting. (The cutlass was initially used for butchering meat and later for close-quarters combat.) The long gun would be fired from the pirate's shoulder, sighting officers and helmsman from high up in the ship's crosstrees. So skilled were buccaneers and pirates with the musket that they could shoot a moving target at 100 yards.

Spanish Main

During the days of the Spanish New World Empire, the mainland of South America bordering the Caribbean Sea and Gulf of Mexico was called the Spanish Main. From as early as the 16th century, the Spanish Main was the point of departure for treasure fleets that carried the enormous wealth (gold, silver, and gems) seized by the Spanish from the Aztecs and Incas. Thus, it was ripe territory for plundering for buccaneers and pirates.

Henry Jennings

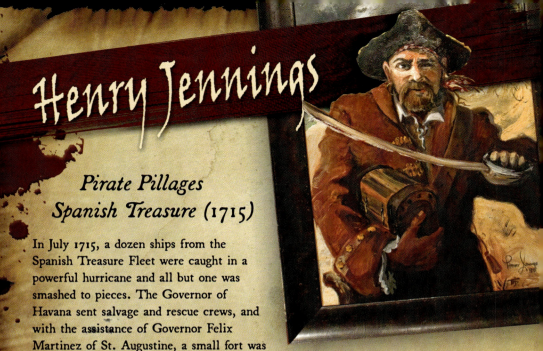

Pirate Pillages Spanish Treasure (1715)

In July 1715, a dozen ships from the Spanish Treasure Fleet were caught in a powerful hurricane and all but one was smashed to pieces. The Governor of Havana sent salvage and rescue crews, and with the assistance of Governor Felix Martinez of St. Augustine, a small fort was erected on the Florida coast under a detachment of 60 soldiers to protect the salvaged silver. Meanwhile, Captain Henry Jennings sailed from Port Royal, Jamaica, and recruited a force of 300 pirates in four ships with a plan to relieve the Spanish of their prized cargo. As darkness descended, his crew ambushed the fort, easily forcing the retreat of the Spanish soldiers. Jennings and his pirate flotilla sailed off with a reported 350,000 pesos or pieces of eight to his new base of operations in New Providence, Bahamas, where he created a pirate stronghold and proclaimed himself Governor.

New Providence

New Providence (present-day Nassau) is a small island just east of Florida lands with the latitude of about 24 degrees north. Here, Captain Henry Jennings, with his newfound wealth and faithful following, proclaimed himself governor and created a pirate stronghold that further fueled the Golden Age of Piracy. New Providence became the new Port Royal. The island was situated in the center of trade lanes between Europe and the West Indies. It had a large protected harbor and lots of rum, food, fresh water, and lumber for refitting vessels. It was said that "When a pirate slept, he didn't dream that when he'd died, he'd gone to heaven, he dreamed that he had once again returned to New Providence".

Pieces of Eight

A piece of eight weighed about 28 grams and contained a very fine quality of silver (92-98%). The coin got its name because it had a nominal value of eight reales, which was a Spanish unit of currency, and was often cut with a sword or dagger into eight pieces or bits to produce smaller currency to purchase rum, clothes, food or fun. One piece of eight was the average monthly salary for a typical sailor at the turn of the 17th century; so imagine the thrill for each pirate crewmember of holding hundreds of pieces of eight as their share of the amazing plunder from Henry Jennings' raid on the 1715 wrecks.

Treasure Chest

The treasure chest was commonly referred to as an iron strongbox. The iron box was extremely strong with its metal panels reinforced with strap work and handmade iron rivets. It weighed anywhere between 150 to 200 pounds and was a wonderful work of art. The ornate face of the chest with the keyhole in the center was for decoration only. The lockplate on the lid was slid open and a large key inserted into the keyhole. Once turned, the key engaged a locking/unlocking mechanism on the interior of the lid that released 10 locking bolts. The two iron latches on the front of the chest were used for padlocking the chest as an additional security measure. Because of the German engineering, once the iron strongbox was discovered aboard a ship, pirates were known to torture their captives to reveal the whereabouts of the chest's key. Otherwise the chest could not be opened to uncover the vast treasure stored within. (The only authentic pirate treasure chest in the world resides at the St. Augustine Pirate & Treasure Museum.)

Charles Vane

Pirate Returns to the Scene of the Crime (1716)

Charles Vane began his career as a pirate under Captain Jennings when he recruited a contingent of more than 300 pirates from his stronghold in Port Royal to raid a Spanish encampment on Florida's eastern coast. Vane and his quartermaster, Calico Jack Rackam (who eventually found fame with his female pirate crew of Anne Bonny and Mary Read), returned to Florida to poach the 1715 wrecks, but their approach was slightly different from Jennings'. Lacking the large army of pirates, Vane wisely avoided attacking the heavily guarded Spanish camp. Instead, he waited until the silver was hauled aboard a rescuing Spanish ship and then attacked as it entered the Florida Straits off the coast of St. Augustine. Vane continued to plunder the American Eastern shoreline where he encountered the notorious Blackbeard for a weeklong bacchanal before meeting his demise at the end of an Admiralty rope.

Pistol Proof

A successful pirate captain needed to be "pistol proof". He had to be an expert at ship handling, crew control, and naval warfare. He also had to exude confidence and exert strong leadership whenever he was in the crew presence, while keeping the hardcore men content and in good spirits. Captaining a pirate ship was like walking a tightrope over a pool of hungry sharks.

Blackbeard

Blackbeard, formerly known as Edward Teach, earned a reputation as the most notorious pirate who ever sailed the American eastern coastline. He was a fearsome sight with an outrageously long bushy black beard braided with colorful ribbons that covered most of his face and chest. When battle called, Blackbeard became a walking arsenal. The large pirate wore a shoulder sling of three pairs of pistols and a cutlass and dagger inserted into his wide belt, and he would place slow-burning matches under his hat. The ghostly smoke encircling his head terrified his prey, who thought the devil himself was attacking them and usually surrendered without a fight. At the height of his career in 1718, Blackbeard commanded a pirate flotilla of four ships and 400 men.

Calico Jack Rackam

Leader of Women Pirates (1716)

Shortly after he plundered the Spanish wrecks as quartermaster under Captain Charles Vane, Calico Jack Rackam challenged Vane's decision to run from a fight with a well-armed French frigate in the Windward Passage. The pirate crew took a vote. They branded Vane a coward, set him adrift aboard an unarmed sloop, and elected Calico Jack captain. While sailing from the pirate paradise of New Providence, Calico Jack met Anne Bonny, who became one of the crew—and his lover. A second female, Mary Read, who disguised herself as a man, also signed the articles of piracy aboard Rackam's ship, *William*. Together, Bonny and Read became infamous, not only because women in the pirate ranks were so rare, but also because of their remarkably bold feats. There is no record of the pirate queens touching the Florida coastline, but then again, they didn't walk onto a hangman's scaffold like their captain either...

Jolly Roger

Pirate flags were flown to strike mortal terror in the hearts and minds of merchant seamen. The flags often featured skulls, crossbones, skeletons, daggers, cutlasses, bleeding hearts, and hourglasses on a red (battle) or black (death) background. Calico Jack Rackam flew a Jolly Roger designed with a skull over crossed swords on a black background. (One of the only surviving Jolly Roger flags is displayed at the St. Augustine Pirate & Treasure Museum.)

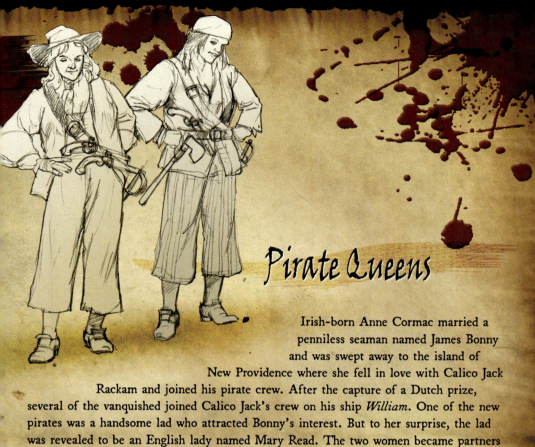

Pirate Queens

Irish-born Anne Cormac married a penniless seaman named James Bonny and was swept away to the island of New Providence where she fell in love with Calico Jack Rackam and joined his pirate crew. After the capture of a Dutch prize, several of the vanquished joined Calico Jack's crew on his ship *William*. One of the new pirates was a handsome lad who attracted Bonny's interest. But to her surprise, the lad was revealed to be an English lady named Mary Read. The two women became partners in crime and were courageous wildcats in battle to the very end. When Calico Jack's ship was attacked off the coast of Jamaica by a well-armed privateer, the men crewmembers were too drunk belowdeck to fight. But the two pirate queens immediately sprung into action with pistols firing and cutlasses slashing until they were captured. Mary died in prison and Anne, pregnant at the time, disappeared from the history books.

No Quarter

When pirates hoisted the red flag, it meant "No Quarter". No mercy would be shown and all souls onboard killed. The captain's call for No Quarter usually resulted after the pirate vessel fired a warning shot and hoisted the Jolly Roger but the prey refused to strike her colors and signal surrender.

Francisco Menendez

Ex-slave Pirate Defends St. Augustine (1741)

In the early 1700s, former slaves were welcomed by the Spanish in St. Augustine as colonists. Many of them, including Francisco Menendez, were set up at Fort Mose just north of St. Augustine to defend against British invasion as front line protection. The fort was destroyed in a bloody battle in 1740 that saved St. Augustine. Menendez then took on a commission as a privateer for the Spanish government and was able to recruit many black volunteers who had formerly served under him at Fort Mose. In 1741, the British ship *Revenge* captured Menendez's vessel and he was given a pirate's welcome: 200 lashes followed by a vinegar and salt bath. He was to be resold as a slave, but instead, Menendez was ransomed and returned to Florida. He helped rebuild the fort and he was once again in command at St. Augustine's Fort Mose.

Cat-o-nine-tails

The "cat" was a multi-tailed whipping device of nine tightly wound and knotted strands of cord attached to a leather-bound piece of wood. To ensure the captain of a pirate ship didn't simply flog men whenever he felt the urge, flogging was only carried out by the ship's quartermaster after a majority vote by the crew and the captain's order to commence. This varied greatly from the procedure aboard a Spanish galleon, Royal Navy vessel or merchant ship where captains had autocratic rule and administered punishment as they deemed necessary—like the sadistic penalty of 200 strokes across Francisco's Menendez's bare back.

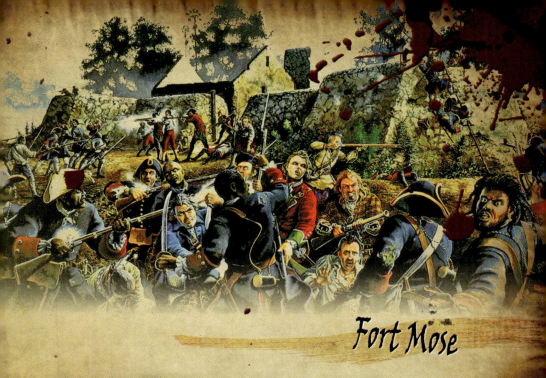

Fort Mose

As early as 1687, the Spanish government offered asylum to British slaves in return for Catholic conversion and a term of four years of service to the Crown. In the 1700s, runaway slaves were taken into the Spanish militia and posted at Gracia Real de Santa Teresa de Mose (Fort Mose), located about two miles north of St. Augustine. It was the first legally sanctioned community of freed slaves in the United States and is now recognized as a National Historic Landmark.

Grub and Grog

Food preservation on a pirate ship was a big problem since food items spoiled and rotted rather quickly, especially considering the humidity and salt air. Meats that were pickled or salted would last for short excursions and island hopping, but voyages over a week required a constant resupply of livestock, fruits, vegetables and fresh water, or else the crew had to rely on washing down hardtack biscuits — that lasted forever but tasted like "digestible leather" — with copious amounts of rum.

Thomas Bell

Dying Pirate Holds his Tongue (1785)

Thomas Bell was shot while committing an "Act of Piracy" at the plantation of Jesse Fish on Anastasia Island. The judge interrogated him but did not learn much from the pirate who had obviously taken an oath of silence. Bell admitted only that he was a crewmember of the schooner *Escape* that last sailed from Charleston, South Carolina. St. Augustine's Spanish Governor Manuel de Zespedes wrote later that day: "Thomas Bell died two hours after he had made his brief declaration, but his body is being exposed on the gallows (of the Castillo) where he would have been hanged within twenty-four hours if he have lived; for, by his own confession it was evident that he had been an accomplice in a flagrant act of piracy".

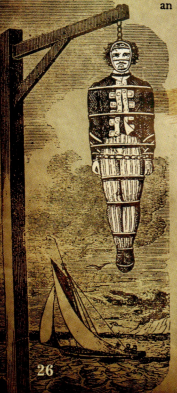

The Gibbet

The sentence for being found guilty of piracy was "to be hanged by the neck till you are dead, dead, dead". The pirate's dead body was usually tarred, chained, and hung from a gibbet or gallows-type structure as a grisly warning to deter other pirates from "going on account". Gibbets were sometimes erected close to the sea's low-water mark and pirates were left dangling until they had been submerged by the tide three times. Other times, like in the famous cases of Captain William Kidd (1701) or Calico Jack Rackam (1720), their bodies hung for much longer.

Anastasia Island

Anastasia Island is an 18-mile long barrier island due east/southeast of St. Augustine. It is separated from the mainland by the Matanzas River. The Spanish built a wooden watchtower on Anastasia Island, which was sighted by Sir Frances Drake in 1586 and then attacked when he came ashore.

Compass & Loadstone

Whether a vessel was navigating from the pirate strongholds of Port Royal or Madagascar to the America's eastern seaboard, the time-honored compass was the most vital navigational tool aboard the ship. Since the needle always points north, pirates could, at minimum, gauge their direction. A lost compass at sea was easily remedied if the ship carried a loadstone. Many captains were known to place their lodestones in decorative mountings to keep them safe, as well as to demonstrate their value.

Louis Aury

Florida's Pirate Governor (1817)

Louis Aury began his naval career in the French Navy, sailed as a privateer for Cartagena in their fight for independence from Spain, and finally flew the black flag as a French corsair in the early 19th century. In 1817, Aury captured Amelia Island in Northeast Florida, just a short sail north of St. Augustine, where he appointed himself commander-in-chief and proclaimed the island an independent republic. Most of the respectable inhabitants fled and Aury took over the area along with 130 mulattoes known as "Aury's blacks", plus an international mixture of South American patriots motivated to plundering and privateering. He died in 1821 when he was thrown from a horse, but was infamously remembered as the pirate who ruled Amelia Island.

Amelia Island

Amelia Island is a 13-mile long island off the coast of northern Florida. It was named after the daughter of England's King George II, but was under the Spanish flag in 1807 when the Jefferson Embargo closed off all United States' ports to foreign shipping—a move that led to the War of 1812. The United States eventually took possession of Amelia Island in trust for Spain, mainly because of Louis Aury's smuggling and pirate activities in 1817. East Florida was eventually ceded to the United States on July 10, 1821.

Privateer or Pirate?

A privateer was a private sailor or warship legally authorized by a country's government with a Letter of Marque to attack enemy ships. The privateer was entitled to keep most of the plunder, including the value of the vessel. During the 17th and 18th centuries, several nations used privateers as an integral part of their naval warfare. But if a peace treaty was signed and the privateer continued to attack vessels, they were labeled pirates. Famous privateers who turned into pirates were Captain William Kidd, Benjamin Hornigold, Blackbeard, and Jean Lafitte.

Pirate Time

Like military or merchant vessels, the custom aboard pirate ships was to divide shipboard duties into regular "watches" — each lasting four hours. Time was determined by a 30-minute sandglass that was turned (restarted) every half hour. The ship's bell rang with each turn, beginning with one stroke half an hour after midnight, and adding an extra stroke every half hour after that. Watches were changed every eight bells — 4:00, 8:00, and 12:00.

ship "Earl Bathurst"
sailing from Liverpool,
wrecked at Pensacola.

1766 Unidentified French ship, commanded by Monsieur Pierre Viaud, was wrecked on the coast of Florida

Billy Bowlegs Ship "Misterio" sank with gold stolen from the Yucatan

1803 Pirate Ship wrecked off
in ambush by disguised British

GULF OF MEXICO

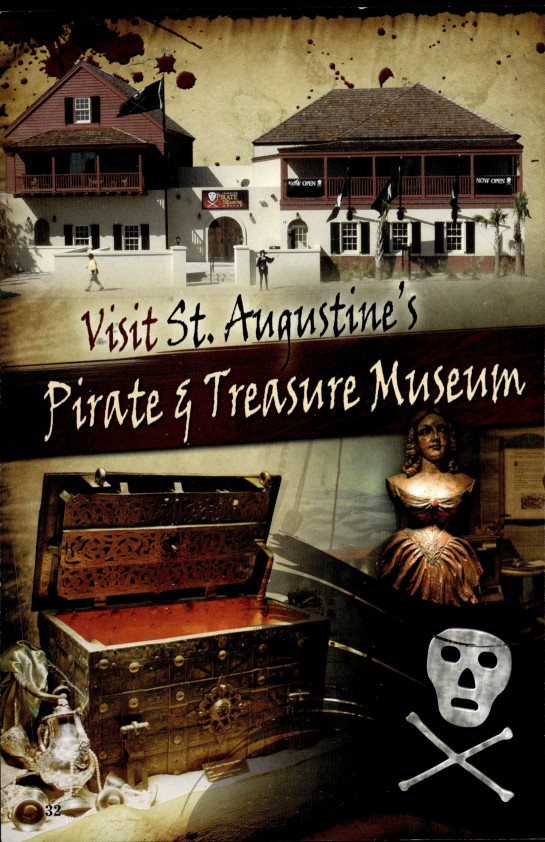